C000172762

Text: *Carl Rogers and Tony Bowerman*

Photographs: *Carl Rogers, Shutterstock, Stewart Smith Photography, Timothy Ball, Linda Lyon, Erwin Neudorfer*

Design: *Carl Rogers*

Northern Eye Books
ISBN 978-0-9553557-5-2

A CIP catalogue record for this book is available from the British Library

www.northerneyebooks.co.uk

First published in 2011 by

Northern Eye Books Limited
Northern Eye Books, Tattenhall, Cheshire CH3 9PX
Email: tony@northerneyebooks.co.uk
For sales enquiries, please call 01928 723 744

Cover: *Sunlit trees, Ullswater*

 Twitter: @CarlMarabooks
@Northerneyeboo
@Top10walks

Contents

England's Largest National Park 4

Top 10 Walks: Lakeside Walks 6

1. **Windermere** 8

2. **Coniston Water** 14

3. **Rydal Water** & **Grasmere** 20

4. **Ullswater** 26

5. **Thirlmere** 32

6. Around **Derwent Water** 38

7. Around **Buttermere** 44

8. Around **Crummock Water** 48

9. Around **Loweswater** 54

10. Around **Ennerdale Water** 58

Useful Information 64

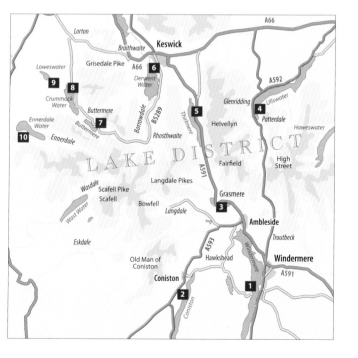

England's Largest National Park

THE LAKE DISTRICT NATIONAL PARK is the largest and most popular of the thirteen National Parks in England and Wales. Created as one of Britain's first National Parks in 1951, its role is to 'conserve and enhance' the natural beauty, wildlife and culture of this iconic English landscape, not just for residents and visitors today but for future generations, too.

Remarkably, the National Park contains every scrap of England's land over 3,000 feet, including its highest mountain, Scafell Pike. Packed within the Park's 885 square miles are numerous peaks and fells, over 400 lakes and tarns, around 50 dales, six National Nature Reserves, and more than 100 Sites of Special Scientific Interest—all publicly accessible on over 1,800 miles of footpaths and other rights of way. It's no surprise then, that the Lake District attracts an estimated 15 million visitors a year.

A calm summer morning at Loweswater

Lakes and Tarns

Lakeland's characteristic lakes and tarns are a legacy of the last Ice Age when vast ice sheets scoured out deep U-shaped valleys and upland combes.

Today, sixteen main lakes and scores of smaller tarns punctuate the National Park. They include England's longest lake (Windermere: 10½ miles long), and its deepest lake (Wast Water: 243 feet deep). Only Windermere, Derwent Water, Coniston Water and Ullswater have regular steamer and ferry services, yet every lake features dramatic waterside walks that will stay in your memory forever.

"Like a fair sister of the sky,
  Unruffled doth the blue lake lie,
  Its mountains looking on."

William Wordsworth, *Complete Poetical Works*, 1819

TOP 10 **Walks:** Lakeside Walks

IT IS GENERALLY AGREED that there are sixteen main lakes and reservoirs in the Lake District National Park. However, some are hard to get to, hemmed in by roads, or otherwise unsuitable for walkers. The ten lakes selected here have been chosen for the excellent walks around or along their shores. Some are sheltered and intimate; others are stark and dramatic. Yet every one of the chosen lakes has a special character and a natural beauty all its own.

Windermere *page 8*

Coniston Water *page 14*

Rydal & Grasmere *page 20*

Ullswater *page 26*

Thirlmere page 32

Derwent Water page 38

Buttermere page 44

Crummock Water page 48

Loweswater page 54

Ennerdale Water page 58

Moored yachts are a common sight on Windermere

Windermere

A fairly easy walk on lanes, forest roads and good paths with views across England's largest lake

What to expect:
Good footpaths, quiet lanes and forest trails. One steep descent

Distance/time: 8.5km/5¼ miles. Allow 2½ hours

Start: National Trust Pay and Display car park near the ferry terminal, 1km east of Far Sawrey. Alternative parking is available 500m along the lane at the start of the walk (also National Trust)

Grid ref: SD 387 954 (alternative SD 387 960)

Ordnance Survey Map: OL 7 *The English Lakes South-eastern area. Windermere, Kendal & Silverdale*

After the walk: Pubs in Near and Far Sawrey

Walk outline
Easy walking on a tarmac lane leads from the Bowness/Far Sawrey ferry terminal along the western shore of the lake through the Claife Estate, now owned by the National Trust. The lane continues as a rough forest road as far as Belle Grange house where it is abandoned in favour of forest paths. These take you over the wooded hills of Claife Heights with wide views out over the lake.

Windermere

At ten and a half miles long and a mile wide, Windermere is both the Lake District's and England's largest lake. It's also the most accessible and most popular of the English Lakes, and ever since the railway reached Windermere in 1847, visitors have flocked to the area in ever-increasing numbers.

Today, Windermere's eastern shore is busy with daytrippers, tourists and boaters. Yet, just a short ferry ride away, much of the quieter wooded western shore is protected by the National Trust. Some lovely walks here will take you to places such as Fell Foot Park, Far Sawrey and Claife Heights.

Moored yacht

Mute swans

The Walk

1. Take the footpath out of the car park signposted to 'Ferry' and 'Latterbarrow via Claife Station'. Ignore the signed path on the left, and continue ahead to the

road. Turn left along the road and, where this swings right to the **ferry**, bear left along the road signposted to 'The Lake Shore'.

2. The road hugs the shore of the lake and soon enters the National Trust's **Claife Estate**.

The National Trust cares for roughly one quarter of the Lake District National Park, and much of the wooded western shore of Windermere, including 2,400 acres of the Claife and Hawkshead Estate.

Pass the National Trust car park (an alternative starting point) and continue along the road, with views out to the right, to wooded **Belle Isle**, Thompson's Holme, Hen Holme and Lady Holme.

3. When the tarmac road ends, a rough forest track continues tight along the shore and on through the trees of **Heald Wood**.

More than 1,000 acres of the Claife Estate are either plantation or semi-natural ancient woodland. The woods hold large numbers of elusive red and roe deer, and are also a good place to spot the increasingly rare native red squirrel.

The track keeps to the left of a caravan site and rises away from the shoreline as you approach the blunt headland of **Slape Scar**.

Continue to **Belle Grange**, the large house on the left at the end of the track.

Ringed by fells: *The unmistakable silhouette of the Langdale Pikes is visible from much of the northern end of WIndermere*

4. Turn left at Belle Grange, on the signed bridleway to 'Hawkshead 3m'. Follow the stone-flagged path that climbs steadily up the hillside onto **Claife Heights**.

Legend claims the lakeside woods here are haunted by a noisy ghost called the 'Claife Crier'. It's said a local ferryman heard a cry of 'boat' one stormy night, rowed across but came back alone and terrified. He died of fear soon afterwards, and his spirit still roams the woods on stormy nights.

When the path levels out, take the footpath on the left signed to 'Far Sawrey via Blind How'. You are now heading back towards the ferry. Ford the stream and climb steadily on a good footpath. Keep right at a fork, passing under power cables and crossing another stream.

5. Walk past the communication masts on the right and continue along the top of **The Heald**, with occasional glimpses of Windermere, far below.

6. At **Low Blind How**, the signed path continues ahead through the woods. A short detour through a gap in the wall

Sheltered waters: *Yachts moored in the bays and sheltered channels between Windermere's islands*

here leads to a crag with dramatic views over the lake, its many islands, and the Troutbeck Fells.

Windermere has more than 18 islands, the largest being 40-acre Belle Isle, which can be seen below. Formerly known as Long Holme, the island was renamed in the late 18th century in honour of Isabella Curwen, the wife of the island's owner.

Return to the main path. Soon the path zigzags and begins to descend near **Low Pate Crag**. Continue ahead between walls, and then over more open ground to finally leave the woods through a gate.

7. Follow the path ahead to a junction, and bear left along a rough track. The track continues, soon between stone walls, to a crossroads.

8. Turn left here on the signposted bridleway to 'Windermere Lake Shore, Ferry'. Follow the track, soon with woods on the right. Look for a path on the right, which leaves the track through a small gate. Pass through a small conifer plantation, then open woodland along the hillside high above Windermere and **Station Scar Woods**.

The path bears left and begins a steep descent, zig-zagging downhill.

Almost at the bottom of the slope, the path passes the ruins of **Claife Station**. Keep ahead at a junction of footpaths a few metres beyond the ruins, and walk down the stone-flagged path and steps to a T-junction. Turn right here, and follow the path back to the car park to complete the walk. ♦

Claife Station

The ruined building above the ferry is called Claife Station. It was built in the 1790s as one of seven 'viewing stations' that promised Georgian tourists the most 'picturesque' views over Windermere. Each window in the drawing room at Claife originally featured different coloured glass to transform the scene outside: yellow for summer, orange for autumn, green for spring, and pale blue for winter.

The Old Man of Coniston, seen from the eastern shore

Coniston Water

An easy walk along a beautiful, wooded section of Coniston Water with a return over undulating, open commmon

What to expect:
Good shoreline footpaths and open woodland. A short section along a road

Distance/time: 12.5km/7¾ miles. Allow 3 hours

Start: Large Pay and Display car park in the centre of Coniston beside the Tourist Information Centre. Toilets are also available beside the Tourist Information Centre

Grid ref: SD 304 976

Ordnance Survey Map: OL 6 *The English Lakes South-western area. Coniston, Ulverston & Barrow-in-Furness*

After the walk: Pubs and cafés in Coniston

Walk outline

Easy walking on good clear paths lead from Coniston village to the shore path. This is a beautiful section of the lake shore—a mix of woods and open common land. The return leg is over the rolling, open land of Torver Commons with its network of footpaths and wide views of the lake and the Coniston Fells.

Coniston Water

Renowned for its mirrored calm, wooded shores and tiny islands, Coniston Water is one of the most beautiful of Cumbria's lakes. It lies in a long, U-shaped glacial valley to the west of Windermere and, at 5 miles long, is the third largest of the Cumbrian lakes. Overlooking the water is the Old Man of Coniston, a fell walkers' favourite rising to 2,635 feet.

Coniston launch

The lake is associated with several famous people including philosopher and artist, John Ruskin, world waterspeed record holder, Sir Donald Campbell, and children's author, Arthur Ransome. Walkers can also benefit from the lake's two year-round ferry services.

Torver Common Wood

The Walk

1. Turn left out of the car park and walk past the church. Turn left at the end of the road and walk over the bridge, passing the garage on the left. Turn left into 'Lake Road' and continue towards the lake. Halfway down the road and immediately before the 'Lake Road Estate', turn right through a kissing gate onto the signed path to 'Torver by Lakeshore'. For the next four kilometres or so, the route follows the long distance **Cumbria Way**.

Coniston has seen several attempts on the world water speed record. Both Sir Malcolm Campbell and his son, Donald, smashed records here between 1939 and 1959. This northern stretch of the lake was the scene of Donald Campbell's tragic death in January 1967 when his jet-powered boat, the 'Bluebird K7', somersaulted and sank after hitting its own wake at more than 300 mph.

2. Keep to the gravel path across the following fields to join the driveway to **Coniston Hall**. Turn left through the gate and walk past the hall and marina.

This unusual Grade II listed mansion dates from 1580 and may incorporate the remains of an earlier peel tower. Owned by the National Trust but privately leased, it's now run as a farm, sailing club, and campsite.

Continue along the access road through the caravan site and camping area.

3. At the far end of the campsite, the road forks. Take the signed footpath to the left, which leads to a path along the lake shore.

Wooded shore: *The western shore of the lake is a beautiful mixture of woods and common, much of it accessible to the public*

On the opposite bank is **Brantwood**, the large rambling house once owned by the Victorian writer, artist and social reformer, John Ruskin. Today, the house is run as a lively museum, art gallery and events centre, open from March to November.

4. When the signed 'Torver' path bears to the right, keep to the shore path instead, soon entering **Torver Common**—an area of open common land and woods.

Originally known as 'Thorvergh', Torver's strange name comes from an Old Norse word meaning 'turf'. In spring, Torver Common Wood is awash with bluebells.

5. Walk on past the **'Torver Jetty'** used by the Coniston launches, and continue ahead on the shore side path through the woods with views out over the lake.

The Coniston Launch Company offers regular cruises on the lake as well as ferry services between Coniston and Brantwood. Alternatively, the National Trust operates the luxurious steam yacht, 'Gondola', throughout the summer months.

Calm and quiet: *A stunning early morning view with flawless reflections in the lake*

6. Beyond the **'Sunny Bank Jetty'**, the path veers right, away from the shore, alongside a wall on the left. Higher up, the path swings to the right, away from the wall. At a fork, the main path keeps right to pass through a kissing gate next to a field gate. Continue along the track to reach the road.

7. Turn right along the road, for about 400 metres, to the garage on the left.

8. Opposite the garage is a lay-by. Take the path from the lay-by to the right to reach a kissing gate that opens onto

'Torver Common'. Follow the path to the left, which soon passes to the left of a small tarn. The faint path continues parallel to the wall on the left.

Where the wall turns left, another small tarn can be seen ahead. To the right of the tarn is a small, grassy rise. Take the path ahead to the top of the rise.

9. Looking ahead, you will see the grassy path descending to pass to the right of the tarn, then continuing ahead towards a second pointed, grassy summit. Follow this path, passing the tarn and the pointed summit, and continue through an area of stunted juniper trees. Soon you will see a wall over to the left. The

path swings to the left, to cross a stream immediately before the wall, then bears right, to run parallel to the wall. Stay on the path beside the wall until it swings left into a small valley, to meet a broad path. Turn right here, and follow the path through a small valley and woods to meet the shore path beside **Torver Jetty**. Retrace the outward route back to Coniston to complete the walk. ♦

Swallows and Amazons

The popular Swallows and Amazons *children's books by Arthur Ransome are largely based on real places around Coniston Water. Although the lake at the heart of their adventures is described only as 'That great lake in the North', it seems to combine elements from both Coniston and Windermere. Coniston's Peel Island becomes 'Wildcat Island' in* Swallows and Amazons, *while Coniston Old Man becomes 'Mount Katchenjunga' in the later* Swallowdale *book.*

Rydal Water and Lanty Scar

Rydal Water & Grasmere

An easy and popular circuit around two of Cumbria's most popular lakes

What to expect:
Good lakeside footpaths and quiet lanes. One short road section

Distance/time: 9.25km/5¾ miles. Allow 2½-3 hours

Start: A small free car park near Rydal. This can be reached by turning left over the little stone bridge immediately before Rydal, approaching from Ambleside. Alternative car parks in Grasmere

Grid ref: NY 365 059

Ordnance Survey Map: OL 7 *The English Lakes South-eastern area. Windermere, Kendal & Silverdale*

After the walk: Pubs and cafés in Grasmere and Rydal

Walk outline

Easy walking on good paths leads beside Rydal Water and along the lower slopes of Loughrigg Fell to Grasmere lake. The path veers away from the shore here to follow a quiet lane to Grasmere village. Roads and lanes lead past Dove Cottage, then good paths with wide views take you high above Rydal Water back to the hamlet of Rydal.

Rydal Water and Grasmere

Rydal Water and Grasmere are forever linked with the Romantic poet, William Wordsworth. Rydal is a stone's throw from Wordworth's former homes of Dove Cottage and Rydal Mount, while nearby Grasmere is a tourist honeypot that draws visitors from around the world. Both lakes are set in a green bowl cradled by Helm Crag, Fairfield, and Loughrigg Fell.

The walk circles these twinned lakes, sometimes rising across the fells, sometimes running around their reedy shores. Places of interest along the way include Dove Cottage and the Wordsworth Museum, Rydal Mount, and the Wordsworth family graves in St Oswald's churchyard.

Helm Crag

Grasmere

Peaceful retreat: *Wordsworth often rowed out to Grasmere's wooded island*

The Walk

1. Turn left out of the car park and walk along the lane, passing '**Cote How'** on the right. Opposite the next house on the left, turn right through the small footgate and follow the path down through the woods.

Leave the woods by a kissing gate and bear left, down towards the lake. Bear left, to enter woods again through a gate. Beyond the woods, continue along the shore of **Rydal Water**.

Across the lake are the lovely, wooded Little Isle and Heron Island. The poet Coleridge described them in 1799 as 'the ovel Island of Trees that lies athwart the Lake ... and Rocky Island ... like the fragment of some huge bridge, now over grown with moss & Trees.'

2. Partway along the lake, the footpath bears left, away from the shore, beside a wall. The path now rises steadily, eventually reaching a high point between **Rydal Water** and **Grasmere**, where you can enjoy striking views over both lakes.

Beyond Grasmere village, at the head of the lake, is **Helm Crag** *(1,298 feet). It's also known as 'The Lion and the Lamb', as the rocks resemble a lion menacing a lamb.*

3. Take the path straight ahead (ignore the path to the left here which traverses the fell above Grasmere, known as 'Loughrigg Terrace'). The path makes a steady descent to the outflow of **Grasmere** where there is a large wooden footbridge on the right.

Don't cross the bridge; instead continue ahead along the shingle shore.

4. At the end of the shingle beach, go through the gate into **Deerbolt Wood.** Continue on the path above the shore with lovely views across the lake towards Helm Crag.

In the foreground is a pretty wooded island often visited by William Wordsworth. Of this island, his friend Coleridge wrote, 'We drank tea the night before I left Grasmere, on the island in that lovely lake, our kettle swung over the fire, hanging from the branch of a Fir Tree'

5. Beyond the woods, continue with fields on the left until the footpath turns left, away from the shore, and rises to join a quiet lane. Turn right along the lane and walk into **Grasmere village**.

Thanks to its associations with the Romantic poet, William Wordsworth (1770-1850), Grasmere is probably the Lake District's most visited village. Famous writers and artists from the past such as Sir Walter Scott, Samuel Coleridge, and John Ruskin also loved this area.

6. In the centre of Grasmere, opposite the church, turn right and follow the road over the bridge and on out of the village.

Sheltered waters: *Grasmere is enclosed by some of Cumbria's best known fells—Helm Crag, Seat Sandal and Heron Pike*

7. At the little roundabout, cross over, and take the lane opposite, passing **Dove Cottage** and the **Wordsworth Museum**, which celebrates his life and works.

8. Follow the rising lane until it levels off by '**How Top'**, on the right. Turn left just after 'How Top' (it's the second lane on the left) along a 'no through road' signposted to 'Alcock Tarn and Coffin Route to Rydal'.

This ancient path over the hills was used for centuries to carry the local dead for burial at St Oswald's Church, in Grasmere.

Follow the lane, passing 'Wishing-Gate House' on the right and continue to the end of the tarmac, where there is a small parking area.

9. The lane continues as an unsurfaced access road to the cottage '**Brockstone'**. Keep to the right of the house, following the footpath ahead to reach open fields with views down to Rydal Water and across to Loughrigg Fell.

As you reach the hamlet of **Rydal**, turn right down the lane to the main road.

Nearby is Rydal Mount, where Wordsworth lived from 1813 until his death in 1850.

At the main road turn right and opposite the **Badger Bar pub**, cross over and follow the path through the gap in the wall, and down the slope to cross the river by the footbridge. Take the path ahead, up the small field, to the kissing gate. Then retrace the outward route to complete the walk. ♦

Wordsworth's home

Jane McIlroy/Shutterstock

Lakeland's most celebrated poet, William Wordsworth, lived at Dove Cottage in Grasmere village from 1799 until 1808. It was here that he produced his finest poems. Now open to the public, Wordsworth's old home was originally an inn called the 'Dove and Olive Bough'. In Wordsworth's day the house enjoyed uninterrupted views over the lake and he famously described Grasmere as 'the loveliest spot that man hath ever found'.

The wooded slopes of Birk Fell, Ullswater

Ullswater

A beautiful walk along the isolated southern shore of Cumbria's second largest lake

Distance/time: 10.75km/6¾ miles. Allow 3-4 hours

Start: Launches run up and down the lake throughout the year and are an ideal way to avoid retracing your steps. Car parking is available at the landing stages (Pay and Display)

Grid ref: NY 390 169

Ordnance Survey Map: OL 5 *The English Lakes North-eastern area. Penrith, Patterdale & Caldbeck*

After the walk: Pubs, cafés and hotels in Glenridding

What to expect:

Clear but undulating paths that are rough underfoot. Some short ascents

Walk outline

The walk starts with a boat trip down the lake to the hamlet of Howtown. From this remote settlement, a good lakeside path heads through open woodland high above the lake to reach the collection of farms at Sandwick. The route continues through ancient woodland as the hillsides steepen. The remaining section in the approach to Patterdale has wide views to the Lakeland giants of Helvellyn and St Sunday Crag.

Ullswater

Ullswater is often favourably compared to Switzerland's Lake Lucerne. Two centuries ago, William Wordsworth praised Ullswater in his *Guide to the Lakes*, 'as having perhaps the happiest combination of beauty and grandeur, which any of the Lakes affords.' The second largest of Cumbria's lakes, Ullswater is shaped like an elongated 'Z', backed by impressive mountain scenery.

Star attractions include Aira Force—Lakeland's most spectacular waterfall, red squirrels in the woods, Wordworth's celebrated lakeside daffodils, and the famous year-round launches.

Ullswater 'steamer'

Wheatear

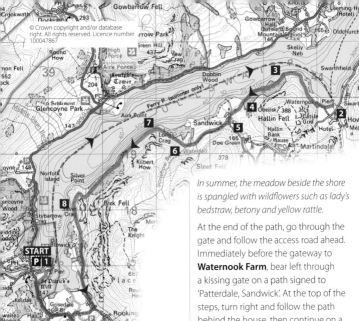

In summer, the meadow beside the shore is spangled with wildflowers such as lady's bedstraw, betony and yellow rattle.

At the end of the path, go through the gate and follow the access road ahead. Immediately before the gateway to **Waternook Farm,** bear left through a kissing gate on a path signed to 'Patterdale, Sandwick'. At the top of the steps, turn right and follow the path behind the house, then continue on a good path high above the lake.

*Up to the left is **Hallin Fell,** where rocky outcrops provide summer nesting sites for meadow pipits and wheatears.*

The path continues through the open semi-natural ancient woodland of **Hallinhag Wood** whose rich bird life includes breeding treecreepers and pied flycatchers.

3. At **Kailpot Crags,** the fine oaks, beeches and Scots pines make perfect foregrounds for long vistas up the lake to the northern end of the **Helvellyn** range.

The Walk

1. From the landing stages in **Glenridding,** take the Ullswater launch to Howtown.

2. From the little pier at **Howtown,** turn right over the wooden footbridge across Fusedale Beck. It's signposted to 'Sandwick'. Follow the footpath around the little bay.

4. Leave the woods by a gate beside a small cove of coarse sand. It's a great spot for a break where children can paddle in the shallow water.

The shoreline ahead is private, so the path heads left, away from the lake, to rise through walled fields.

5. As you approach **Sandwick,** bear left beside Boardale Beck and follow the path across the wooden footbridge and turn left up the road.

Across the lake: *Looking across Ullswater to Glenridding and St Sunday Crag*

Sandwick is a remote hamlet in a beautiful setting on the shore of the lake. Lying at the end of narrow country lanes, its handful of cottages and old farms seem frozen in time.

Beyond the last house (appropriately named 'Townend Cottage'), bear right onto the fell path again. The path contours the fellside high above the walled fields.

6. Cross a footbridge below the waterfall of **Scalehow Force**, visible up to the left, and continue on the path beside the wall.

Mountain lake: *Ullswater is dominated by St Sunday Crag, Helvellyn and Raise*

The waterfall was formed where the Scalehow Beck plunges over a geological fault between hard Borrowdale Volcanics and softer Skiddaw Slates.

7. Soon the path overlooks the lake again and rises to a viewpoint on **Long Crag**.

Across the lake are Gowbarrow, Aira Point and the 19th-century hunting lodge of Lyulph's Tower.

The path crosses scree slopes above the lake. As you approach **Silver Point**, the path forks. Keep ahead here, ignoring the pitched path that rises to the left.

Silver Point overlooks tiny Norfolk Island, previously called House Holm. Today, it's a favourite roost for cormorants. There are good views to the head of the lake, too, to the high fells of St Sunday Crag and Helvellyn.

8. The path continues past the pines on **Purse Point**, then runs beside the walled fields above **Blowick**, the rambling house close to the shore.

Further along, the views embrace Helvellyn's lofty neighbours, Dollywaggon and Nethermost Pike .

The path broadens into a well established farm track as you near the southern end of the lake. Continue to **Side Farm** where a right turn immediately beside the farmhouse takes you along the farm drive, over Goldrill Beck, to the main road on the edge **Patterdale**.

9. Turn right along the road and follow it back to the landing stage at **Glenridding** to complete the walk. ♦

Wordsworth and Ullswater

Wordsworth's best-known poem, I Wandered Lonely as a Cloud, *contains the lines 'When all at once I saw a crowd, A host of golden daffodils; Beside the lake, beneath the trees, Fluttering and dancing in the breeze'. The poem was inspired by a walk that Wordsworth and his sister took along Ullswater's western shore in April 1802. To see the daffodils today, visit Wordsworth Point, near Glencoyne Bay.*

Thirlmere and Raven Crag

Thirlmere

A moderate walk along a short, wooded section of the shore with a return by lower fellsides

What to expect:
Good footpaths and forest trails. One steep ascent and a busy road crossing

Distance/time: 7.5km/4¾ miles. Allow 2-3 hours

Start: Large Pay and Display car park (Swirls Car Park) for Helvellyn, situated on the A591 Ambleside to Keswick road approximately half way along the eastern side of Thirlmere

Grid ref: NY 316 169

Ordnance Survey Map: OL 5 *The English Lakes North-eastern area. Penrith, Patterdale & Caldbeck*

After the walk: Nearest pub: Kings Head, Thirlspot

Walk outline

Forest roads and paths leads along the shore of Thirlmere to Great How. Here you have the choice of a short steep climb to the top of Great How for a grand view of the lake and its surrounds or to continue on the low level route. Return is made via low fellside paths high above Thirlspot with panoramic views. Paths are excellent throughout.

Thirlmere

Thirlmere is one of the Lake District's two man-made lakes. The 3½ mile long reservoir was created in the 1890s to supply water for Manchester's expanding population. As the water level rose behind the dam, it submerged two small lakes called Leathes Water and Wythburn Water, several farms, two inns, and the ancient hamlets of Armboth and Wythburn.

Thirlmere's encircling woods were originally planted to reduce erosion. Today, they provide sheltered waterside walks with views across the lake. Along the way are Dalehead Hall, Great How summit's panoramic views and, for the lucky few, a glimpse of a red squirrel.

Evening sun on Raise

Buzzard

Spring woods: *Following the wooded path beside Thirlmere at the start of the walk*

The Walk

1. From the Swirls Car Park, cross the main road to the layby and car park **(Station Coppice)** opposite. Two gates leave the car park. Ignore the righthand gate, which leads to a viewpoint and short circular walk. Instead, go through the lefthand gate and follow the surfaced path beside the stream down towards the lake.

2. The path bends to the right just before the water to run parallel with the shore. When the track swings to the right again, bear left onto a much narrower signed footpath that continues along the lakeshore.

3. The path winds through open broadleaf woodland, a lovely mix of oak, beech and birch.

The Thirlmere woods are home to Britain's largest mammal, the red deer. The landowners, United Utilities, have also declared the woods a red squirrel refuge, and set up a squirrel-watching hide above the nearby Swirls Car Park.

Soon, the path passes **Dalehead Hall** up to the right.

Now a comfortable hotel with views across the lake, Dalehead Hall dates back to the 16th century. From 1577 to 1877, the hall was the ancestral home of the Leathes family. But when the estate was bought by Manchester Corporation as the site of their new reservoir, the hall became the summer residence of the Lord Mayor of Manchester. It became a private hotel in 1985.

Continue along the wooded shore to reach a broad track that joins from the right. Follow this to the left, rising alongside a wall on the left. Turn left through a gate and keep to the track as it rises high above the lake, which glints through the trees down to the left.

4. As you approach the wooded hill of Great How, the track swings to the right and you have a choice. To continue the walk, follow the track around to the right. Alternatively, to experience the impressive views from **Great How**, bear left onto a clear path that leaves the track on the bend.

The **Great How** path climbs steeply through the woods to the summit, which has been cleared of trees to give a 360-degree panorama over the lake and surrounding fells.

The view takes in much of Thirlmere, stretching away south to the pass of Dunmail Raise. The rounded tops of Watson's Dodd, Stybarrow Dodd, Raise, White Side and Low Man on Helvellyn lie to the east, while Skiddaw and Blencathra fill the northern skyline.

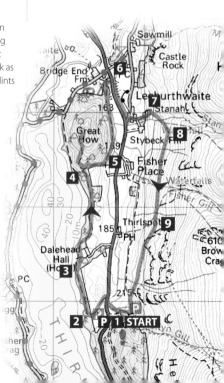

Quiet waters: *Thirlmere is surrounded by pine woods, and overlooked by Helvellyn*

5. Retrace your steps down to the track at the foot of the hill, and turn left.

The track soon begins to descend and, lower down, swings left around the base of **Greathow Wood** to reach the main road (the A591).

6. Turn right along the road and, opposite the St. John's in the Vale lane, cross over. Turn left along the lane here and, within a few metres, turn right along **Stanah Lane**, beside the recreation hall.

7. Follow the rising access road, passing a farm on the right. At the top of the road, cross the ladder stile in the wall ahead, signposted to 'Sticks Pass'. Take the path up the field, to cross a stile by a water leat. Continue the climb, to go through a kissing gate and cross a footbridge over the cascading stream. Beyond the bridge, walk ahead for a few metres, then turn left up to where the path forks.

8. Bear right at the fork, and follow the path that contours the hillside beside the wall on the right.

Keep ahead at a fork in the path, soon crossing a footbridge over the stream.

9. At the next T-junction, keep ahead again, ignoring the righthand path that descends to Thirlspot Farm. Eventually you reach the start of the popular Thirlspot **Helvellyn path**.

This is one of the most popular routes on the mountain due to its easy access.

Turn right here, then left over the footbridge to reach the car park, to complete the walk. ♦

Thirlmere dam

Completed in 1894, the Thirlmere dam rises 65 feet above the old streambed and holds back around 9 billion gallons of water. It's constructed of large rocks embedded in concrete, and faced with masonry. Today, Thirlmere still supplies Manchester through a 100-mile long Victorian aqueduct. Powered only by gravity, the tunnels and pipes carry water to the distant city at a stately three miles an hour.

On the jetty at Hawes End, Derwent Water

Around **Derwent Water**

A long but straightforward circuit of one of Lakeland's most beautiful and spectacular lakes

What to expect:

Good lakeside and forest footpaths, one short road section. No ascents or descents

Distance/time: 11.75km/7½ miles. Allow 3-4 hours

Start: Large Pay and Display car park adjacent to the Theatre by the Lake, Keswick. Or car parks in Keswick and follow signs to the Theatre by the Lake

Grid ref: NY 265 229

Ordnance Survey Map: OL 4 *The English Lakes North-western area. Keswick, Cockermouth & Wigton*

After the walk: Pubs, cafés and restaurants in Keswick

Walk outline
Beginning with a boat trip across to Nichol End, good paths lead along the western shore, through the wooded parkland of Brandelhow and Manesty. At the head of the lake, a footbridge crosses the River Derwent followed by a short road section. The beautiful bays around Friar's Crag make a fine end to the circuit. The Derwent launches run daily and can be used to shorten the walk from any of the five stages around the lake.

Derwent Water
Ringed by magnificent fells and shoreside woods, Derwent Water is sometimes dubbed the 'Queen of the Lakes'. The third largest of the Cumbrian lakes, it stretches for three miles between the lakehead market town of Keswick in the north and beautiful Borrowdale in the south.

Regular motor launches leave from Keswick all year round, dropping off and picking up passengers at jetties around the lake. Combining an inexpensive boat trip with a leisurely walk along the tree-lined shore makes for a lovely half day, especially when combined with a lakeside picnic, paddle or swim in warm weather.

Derwent launch

Calfclose sculpture

Wooded shore: *The stunted, bare-rooted pines of Brandelhow Park frame a distant view of Blencathra*

The Walk

1. Turn left out of the car park and walk down to the landing stages. Take a launch across the lake to **Nichol End**.

2. From the **Nichol End** jetty, walk up the access road past the shop and café. Turn left along the drive immediately behind the café. Bear right off the drive, opposite a house on the left, and walk along a wide forestry track.

At a T-junction, turn left along the driveway to '**Lingholm**' and take the signed footpath to the right of the gateway (signed to 'Catbells'). Follow the path ahead through the woods.

Leave the woods by a gate and walk across a field, with **Catbells** rising ahead. Cross a footbridge and take the rising footpath ahead into the woods again.

At the end of the path, a gate leads onto an access road. Turn left along the road (ignore the first left) and in about 50 metres, bear left, off the road, onto a path signed to **'Hawes End Jetty'**, which leads down to the lake shore.

3. Follow the path to the right along the shore. After a stile, the path moves away from the shore to join a well-made gravel footpath. Head left, along the path, which soon swings left back towards the lake. Immediately after a gate, turn sharp left onto a path that leads back to the shore again at **Otterbield Bay**.

Continue along the shore path, to join the main path again. Go through the gate ahead and continue along the shore—a lovely section of small bays and wooded headlands.

4. Pass the launch jetty at **Brandlehow** and, a little further on, skirt an area of old mining spoil. The right of way passes **'Brandlehow'** house, then bears left down the access track. At a fork, keep right and at the next cottage on the right, bear left, off the track, on a footpath that leads back down to the lake shore again at **Abbot's Bay**.

5. Follow the path ahead through the woods of **Manesty Park**. Immediately before the path leaves the woods, bear left to cross a stile on the edge of the water. Follow the path around the next wooded headland.

The path eventually joins the main footpath again where boardwalks carry it over the boggy area where the **River Derwent** enters the lake.

Mirror calm: *Skiddaw is reflected in the calm waters of Calfclose Bay*

Turn left, and follow the boardwalks to cross the footbridge over the river. Continue ahead to reach the road.

6. Turn left and walk along the road past the **Lodore Falls Hotel**. There is a landing stage on the left just before the bridge.

Immediately before the **Mary Mount Hotel**, take the path on the right that runs parallel to the road.

At the **Kettlewell** car park, cross the road and take the shore path again. A permissive path heads round **Barrow Point**. Beyond the headland, the road runs tightly beside the lake. Although it is possible to continue along the shore, it becomes increasingly rocky. It's better to follow the road to the next wooded headland.

7. Drop down to the shore again and walk round into **Calfclose Bay**. Continue on the lakeside path, passing through the ancient yew trees on the next headland. Open fields follow, and as you approach cottages, keep to the right along the access drive. Within 250 metres, turn left through a gate and follow the path through **The Ings**, an area of wooded wetland.

8. The path emerges from the woods opposite wooded **Lord's Island**, then passes through National Trust land at **Strandshag Bay.** Pause here to enjoy the classic views across the lake to **Catbells**, set against the wooded foreground of **Friar's Crag**. Continue past Friar's Crag to eventually reach the road end. The road leads back to the landing stages to complete the walk. ♦

Derwent Isle

Derwent Isle is the only one of Derwent Water's four islands inhabited today. Hidden among the isle's trees is an intriguing 18th-century Italianate house owned by the National Trust but now leased as a private home. Its original owner, Henry Marshall, used to entertain the founders of the National Trust on the island, and today it's open to the public on just five days a year.

The famous Buttermere pines at the head of the lake

Around **Buttermere**

An easy circuit of a beautiful lake in a quiet corner of the Lake District

What to expect:

Good lakeside footpaths, almost entirely on the level. One section on rocky, uneven ground

Distance/time: 6.5km/4 miles. Allow 2-3 hours

Start: In the village of Buttermere where there are two National Trust car parks

Grid ref: NY 174 170

Ordnance Survey Map: OL 4 *The English Lakes North-western area. Keswick, Cockermouth & Wigton*

After the walk: Bridge Hotel and Fish Hotel, Buttermere. Tea room, Buttermere

Walk outline

The shoreline circuit of Buttermere is a deservedly popular and easy walk with good footpaths all the way round. It's level throughout, apart from a short, uneven section close to Hassness house where the path has been cut from the steep rocks and passes through a short tunnel.

Buttermere

Buttermere is famous for its classic combination of lake and mountain scenery. The lake sits in a deep valley surrounded by woods and towering crags, overlooked by High Stile, Red Pike, Fleetwith Pike and Haystacks. Originally a single lake, Buttermere and neighbouring Crummock Water are now separated by a belt of lush meadows.

St James' Church

The easy, level path around the lake is perfect for families and provides plenty of places to picnic, paddle or play. En route, the path passes through a short tunnel. Look out, too, for locally-made ice cream at Syke Farm, and Alfred Wainwright's touching memorial in St James' Church.

The Buttermere pines

The Walk

1. From the little bridge in the centre of **Buttermere** village, take the road beside the Bridge Hotel, and keep to the left of the Fish Hotel along a gravel farm road.

2. Immediately after the gate just before the lake, turn right to cross the footbridge over **Buttermere Dubs**, the river flowing out of Buttermere. Cross a second footbridge over Sourmilk Gill, the stream that tumbles down the steep hillside above.

Go through the hand gate and bear left on the broad path that hugs the lake shore. The path continues through **Burtness Wood,** which clothes the lower slopes of High Crag and High Stile.

There are good views from occasional breaks in the trees across to Hassness house in its wooded gardens, and up to Fleetwith Pike high above the valley head.

3. After Burtness Wood and just before you reach the head of the lake, the path splits. Keep ahead here on the lakeside trail (ignore the path that climbs diagonally up to the right, heading for Haystacks and Scarth Gap).

Continue through a kissing gate and cross the footbridge over Warnscale Beck. Follow the path ahead, across the wide valley floor, to reach the road beside **Gatesgarth Farm**.

4. Turn left, and walk along the road to reach the lake again. Stay with the road as it swings to the right, and then to the left, along the shore. A gate on the left marks the start of the shore path again.

Follow the path down to, and then along, the shore, with wonderful

Favourite fell: *Haystacks, the favourite fell of Alfred Wainwright at the head of Buttermere*

views ahead to High Stile and back towards the great prow of Fleetwith Pike.

5. The path below the large house of **Hassness** has been cut into the rock right along the water's edge. Immediately after this, the path passes through a short tunnel where the rocks are at their steepest. Beyond the tunnel, the path runs along the shore through fields and open woods.

6. At the end of the lake, go through a gate on the left, and walk back along the shore to rejoin the outwards route, just before **Buttermere Dubs**. Retrace your steps back to Buttermere village to complete the walk. ♦

Wainwright's Memorial
The celebrated author and fellwalker Alfred Wainwright made the area around Buttermere famous with his hand-written and hand-illustrated book, The Western Fells: the seventh volume of his iconic Pictorial Guides to the Lakeland Fells. *There is a memorial to him set into a windowsill in nearby St James' Church. The window looks out over Haystacks—probably Wainwright's favourite fell—where his ashes were scattered in 1991.*

Red Pike and Ling Crag reflected in Crummock Water

Around **Crummock Water**

A rugged circuit of one of the most dramatic lakes in the Lake District

What to expect:
Unspoilt paths, stony and wet in places. Mainly on the level, with one short ascent

Distance/time: 12.75km/8 miles. Allow 3½ hours

Start: In the village of Buttermere where there are two National Trust car parks.

Grid ref: NY 174 170

Ordnance Survey Map: OL 4 *The English Lakes North-western area. Keswick, Cockermouth & Wigton*

After the walk: Bridge Hotel and Fish Hotel, Buttermere. Detour to the Kirkstile Inn, Loweswater

Walk outline
From Buttermere village, easy walking on good paths leads to Crummock Water with its superb views. A short ascent onto the shoulder of Rannerdale Knott is followed by a long descent to regain the shore at Lanthwaite Woods. Woodland paths around this lovely section of the shore are followed by an optional detour to Scale Force, Lakeland's highest waterfall.

Crummock Water
Rugged, unspoilt Crummock Water lies between Buttermere and Loweswater in the Lake District's quiet, northwest corner. Flanked by Rannerdale Knotts and mighty Grasmoor to the east, and with the steep slopes of Mellbreak plunging into its clear waters along the western shore, Crummock Water really is an atmospheric location.

Lanthwaite Woods

Every part of the path around the lake passes through dramatic scenery. Along the way, look out for spring bluebells at Rannerdale, red squirrels in Lanthwaite and Low Park woods, the curious lakeside peninsula of Low Ling Crag, and the impressive Scale Force waterfall.

Low Ling Crag

The Walk

1. From the centre of **Buttermere** village, by the bridge, take the road beside the Bridge Hotel. At the Fish Hotel, bear right, following the road alongside the stream and through the National Trust car park.

2. At the end of car park, go through the kissing gate on the right and continue on the footpath beside **Mill Beck**. Go through a small gate and walk across the field towards the lake.

3. Well before you reach the shore, cross a footbridge over the beck on the right, and turn left. Follow the path beside the wall through a small wood. Turn left at a kissing gate, and walk down to **Crummock Water**. Follow the path to the right, along the shore.

From here there are lovely views down the lake to the slopes of Mellbreak, which plunges 300 metres to the shore. As Wainwright observes, 'No pairing of hill and lake in Lakeland have a closer partnership than these'.

4. When you reach the road, cross over and take the footpath opposite, which cuts left through the bracken around the lower slopes

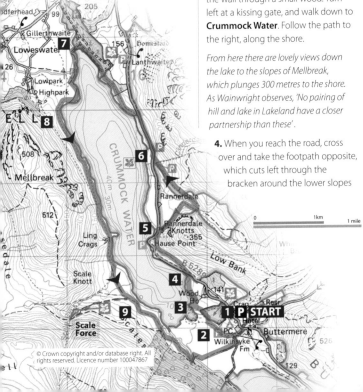

Splash of colour: *Bluebells carpet the secluded Rannerdale valley in early spring*

of **Rannerdale Knotts**. As you round the shoulder of Rannerdale Knotts, the impressive profile of Grasmoor comes into view, along with a grand panorama over the northern half of the lake.

5. Take the pitched path down to the road and turn right. Almost immediately, turn right again, off the road, where it bears left. Follow the path through a small parking area and on beside the wall. Keep beside the wall, until you pass through a kissing gate. The path now

veers right, away from the wall into the attractive **Rannerdale** valley.

Follow the path beside the stream to a footbridge, on the left. Cross the bridge and take the good path to the left. This contours above fields down to the left to eventually reach a car park.

6. Turn right along the lane. At a kissing gate on the left, turn left and follow the path down to the lake shore. Follow the path to the right, close to the water's edge, to eventually enter the pines of **Lanthwaite Wood**. Continue through the woods, passing a small boathouse.

Morning calm: *Mellbreak, the High Stile group and distant Great Gable cast flawless reflections in Crummock Water*

Near the end of the lake, keep left at a fork where there are seats.

This is a good place to stop and take in the superb views back up the lake to High Stile and Red Pike. The lower summit of Rannerdale Knotts completes one of the loveliest mountain views in England.

7. Cross the outflow from the lake by two footbridges and stay on the lakeside path with a superb view of Grasmoor rising over 700 metres above.

Cross another footbridge and continue past a small pumping station. Rejoin the shore and walk around the next headland to a beautiful shingle bay, sheltered below the steep slopes of **Mellbreak**.

8. From the bay, the lakeside path continues, with grand views ahead, up the lake to **Low Ling Crag**, a little peninsula that juts into the lake.

Further along the shore, the path crosses **Scale Beck** by a wooden footbridge. Keep ahead after the bridge, on a broad footpath, to cross a second stream and continue over more boggy ground.

9. At a T-junction turn left to return directly to Buttermere. (To visit **Scale Force**, turn right here, alongside the stream. It is a straightforward there-and-back detour of around 2km/1¼ miles.)

As you approach **Buttermere**, cross a stone bridge on the left, and follow the farm road back to Buttermere village to complete the walk. ♦

Scale Force

The highest waterfall in the Lake District, Scale Force plunges 170 feet in a single drop, with two smaller falls each of around 20 feet. It's hidden in a deep, tree-lined gorge on the northern flank of Red Pike, above Crummock Water. In Victorian times, launches brought sightseers across the lake to see what Wordsworth described as 'a fine chasm with a lofty, but slender, fall of water'.

A peaceful morning at Loweswater

Around **Loweswater**

An easy circuit of a small but pretty lake in a quiet corner of the Lake District

What to expect:

Woodland paths and quiet lanes. Mainly level walking with one steep ascent

Distance/time: 6.75km/4¼ miles. Allow 2 hours

Start: Layby at the western end of Loweswater lake on the minor lane linking the hamlet of Loweswater and Mockerkin

Grid ref: NY 118 224

Ordnance Survey Map: OL 4 *The English Lakes North-western area. Keswick, Cockermouth & Wigton*

After the walk: Kirkstile Inn, Loweswater

Walk outline

A steep climb on farm access roads leads to the old fell road high on the slopes of Low Fell with superb views of Loweswater and its surrounds. The fell road is followed back down through woods to the lane by the lake shore. Lanes, farm roads and forest tracks leads around the southern shore of the lake and on through Holme Wood. Good field paths are used to complete the route.

Loweswater

Hidden away in the top, northwest corner of the Lake District, sleepy Loweswater promises peace and quiet even in the height of summer. As the smallest of the lakes in the Buttermere valley, it also attracts fewer visitors than either Crummock Water or busy Buttermere.

Roughly a mile long by half a mile wide, and with a quiet road, cart tracks and paths around the shore, Loweswater provides the perfect, easy lakeside circuit for walkers. Along the way, look out for red squirrels and Holme Force waterfall in Holme Woods, or hire a traditional clinker built rowing boat from the National Trust at Watergate Farm.

Kirkstile Inn, Loweswater

Roe deer

The Walk

1. Opposite the layby is an access road signposted to 'Myre Syke' and 'Public Bridleway to **Mosser Fell Road**'. Follow the road as it rises steeply to a sharp lefthand bend. Ignore the road ahead to 'Myre Syke only'. Immediately after the bend, bear right onto a fenced path, which continues the climb to join the old fell road.

2. Turn sharp right along the fell road, now little more than a farm track. Follow the lane on its gentle descent back to **Loweswater**.

The easy walking will allow you to take in the wide views down to the lake with its beautiful woods backed by the fells of Carling Knott.

3. At the road turn left. In around 1.25km/¾ mile, turn right down the lane signed to 'Loweswater 0.8 miles'.

4. Follow the lane until it forks at the Loweswater National Trust sign. Bear right through a small car park, over the cattle grid, and continue along a farm access road towards the lake.

5. Just before **Watergate Farm**, bear right, off the track, across grass to rejoin the track by a gate that leads into **Holme Wood**. Go through the gate and follow the track ahead, which stays close to the lake shore on the right.

6. When you reach a small stone hut, bear right, off the forest track, and follow a narrower footpath that continues along the wooded shore.

The little shingle beach beside the hut is a good place to linger with its lovely views up the lake to the fells of Whiteside, Grasmoor, Whiteless Pike and Mellbreak.

Golden glow: *The autumn hues of Holme Wood are reflected in Loweswater*

Continue on the lakeside footpath beyond the hut, crossing a footbridge over **Holme Beck**. At the far side of the woods the path swings left to rejoin the forest track. Turn right and go through the gate out of the woods.

7. Follow the track between open fields above the lake. At **Hudson Place**, go through the gate and turn right down the access road. In about 300 metres, take the signed footpath over the stile on the right. Follow the footpath ahead across the field. Boardwalks take you over marshy ground and a footbridge leads over the stream. Trace the footpath through the following fields to the lane, to complete the walk. ◆

Red squirrels

Beatrix Potter's Squirrel Nutkin made the red squirrel a Lake District icon. Today, the northern Lakes—and especially Holme Wood, at Loweswater—are among the best places in England to see our native red squirrels. Smaller and daintier than their American grey cousins, red squirrels have russet fur and tufted ears. Watch out for the squirrels' large nests or 'dreys' high in the trees.

Angler's Crag and Ennerdale Water

Around **Ennerdale Water**

A clear but rugged circuit of a wild and beautiful lake in a quiet corner of the Lake District

What to expect:
Forest roads and rocky paths with a short scramble. Not suitable for young children

Distance/time: 11km/6¾ miles. Allow 3 hours

Start: Forestry Commission car park at the end of the public road beside the lake at Bowness Knott

Grid ref: NY 109 153

Ordnance Survey Map: OL 4 *The English Lakes North-western area. Keswick, Cockermouth & Wigton*

After the walk: The Shepherds Arms, at Ennerdale Bridge

Walk outline

A clear forest road leads to the head of the lake where a farm road crosses the river. A rocky footpath continues along the southern shore of the lake, edging around Angler's Crag by a short, easy scramble. The final section is by an easy, level shore path with good views of the surrounding fells.

Ennerdale Water

Unspoilt and increasingly wild, Ennerdale Water occupies a secluded valley in the far northwest corner of the Lake District. It's the only Cumbrian lake without a public road running alongside it; and even in high season, Ennerdale is the perfect place to escape the pressures of modern life and get closer to nature. Since 2003, the valley's landowners have deliberately allowed it to revert gradually to wilderness.

With over 30 miles of forest tracks and paths, Ennerdale offers outstanding opportunities for walking, biking, riding and climbing. The sheltered circular walk around the lake is mostly flat and easy except for a brief section over Angler's Crag which requires a short scramble.

Steeple

Dipper

The Walk

1. From the **Bowness Knott** car park at the end of the public road, follow the forestry road along the northeastern side of the lake.

The remote Ennerdale Valley has a wild, Scottish feel to it. Its deep glacial lake is ringed by pine plantations and high fells, with Pillar, one of the loveliest Lakeland fells, rising impresssively at the head of the valley.

Pillar takes its name from Pillar Rock, the large buttress high on the northern slopes. Pillar Rock fascinated early rock climbers as

the only Lakeland summit requiring actual climbing. John Atkinson of Crowfoot, Ennerdale, made the first recorded ascent in 1826. His route is known as the Old West Route, and is still climbed regularly today.

2. At the east end of the lake, continue along the road until you reach a large concrete bridge across the **River Liza**, on the right.

The forest road continues for another 7 kilometres/4½ miles to the valley head and an isolated shepherd's bothy called the Black Sail Hut. It's the most remote Youth Hostel in Cumbria.

Watch for dippers along the river, which is also the spawning ground for Ennerdale's rare arctic char.

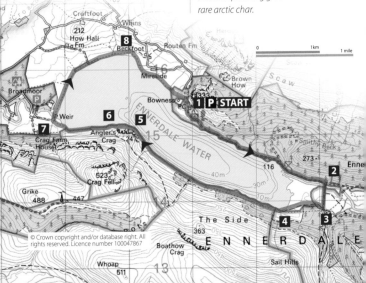

Wild valley head: *Pillar, Steeple and Scoat Fell seen from the approach to Angler's Crag*

Cross the bridge and follow the broad track across the flat valley bottom towards the conifer plantations.

Ennerdale Forest was largely planted between 1926 and 1950, using a mixture of non-native conifers including Norway spruce, Sitka spruce, and European and Japanese larch. Today, it's home to elusive red squirrels, roe deer and, perhaps, even pine martens.

3. Don't enter the plantation ahead.

Instead, immediately before the large gate at the end of the track, turn right through a kissing gate and follow the permissive path down towards the lake. Partway down the field, go through a kissing gate on the left and continue beside a wall on the left.

4. Cross a footbridge to reach the lakeside path. Follow this good path—pitched in places—along the shore, first through the woods, and then across the open fell for almost 2.5 km/1½ miles.

There are good views across the lake from this path but things improve dramatically

Mirror calm: *Great Borne and Bowness Knott cast flawless reflections on a calm morning*

once you leave the lakeside trees. Looking back up the lake, there are superb views in clear weather to Pillar, Scoat Fell, and the shapely Steeple.

5. The path begins a gentle climb as you approach **Angler's Crag**, which has been visible for most of the walk. Despite first appearances, there is a clear path around this rocky headland.

The path rises above steep screes, requiring a little care, before you reach the first rocks. You may need a steadying hand here and there, and there are a few places where the short drop may make some people feel uncomfortable. Children should be closely supervised.

6. Once over these rock steps, the clear path returns to the shoreline and there are no further complications for the rest of the walk.

7. Cross the footbridge where the **River Ehen** flows out of the lake, and follow the clear gravel path ahead. This meets the shore again by a second, smaller wooden footbridge.

Ennerdale Water takes its name from the River Ehen, but was previously called 'Brodewater' or 'Broadwater'. The

unpolluted lake supplies Cumbria's nearby coastal towns with drinking water.

8. When the footpath veers away from the shore, turn right after a gate to regain the path along the water's edge.

When fields on the left give way to rough bracken, take the path to the left that rises past a small cottage to reach the car park, to complete the walk. ♦

Rewilding Ennerdale

'Wild Ennerdale' is the UK's first rewilding project. In a groundbreaking vision for the valley's future, Ennerdale's primary landowners agreed in 2003 to 'allow the evolution of Ennerdale as a wild valley for the benefit of people, relying more on natural processes to shape its landscape and ecology'. As forest tracks become overgrown and the river reverts to its natural course, rare wildlife is returning too.

Useful Information

Cumbria Tourism
Cumbria Tourism's official website covers everything from accommodation and events to attractions and adventure. **www.golakes.co.uk**

Lake District National Park
The Lake District National Park website also has information on things to see and do, plus maps, webcams and news. **www.lakedistrict.gov.uk**

Tourist Information Centres
The main TICs provide free information on everything from accommodation and travel to what's on and walking advice.

Ambleside	01539 432 582	tic@thehubofambleside.com
Bowness	01539 442 895	bownesstic@lake-district.gov.uk
Coniston	01539 441 533	mail@conistontic.org
Keswick	01768 772 645	keswicktic@lake-district.gov.uk
Penrith	01768 867 466	pen.tic@eden.gov.uk
Ullswater	01768 482 414	ullswatertic@lake-district.gov.uk
Windermere	01539 446 499	windermeretic@southlakeland.gov.uk

Steamers and Ferries
Four lakes have regular, year round 'steamers', launches or ferries.

Windermere	01539 443 360	www.windermere-lakecruises.co.uk
		info@windermere-lakecruises.co.uk
Derwentwater	01768 772 263	www.keswick-launch.co.uk
		info@keswick-launch.co.uk
Coniston	01539 441 288	www.nationaltrust.org.uk/gondola
		gondola@nationaltrust.org.uk
	01768 775 753	www.conistonlaunch.co.uk
		info@conferry.co.uk
Ullswater	01768 482 229	www.ullswater-steamers.co.uk
		enquiries@ullswater-steamers.co.uk

Weather
Five day forecast for the Lake District: 0844 846 2444
www.lakedistrict.gov.uk/weatherline